The Fibromyalgia
Cookbook

The Fibromyalgia Cookbook

More Than 120 Easy & Delicious Recipes

Shelley Ann Smith

FOREWORD BY ALISON BESTED, M.D.,
AND ALAN C. LOGAN, N.D.

CUMBERLAND HOUSE
NASHVILLE, TENNESSEE

Published by
Cumberland House Publishing, Inc.
431 Harding Industrial Drive
Nashville, TN 37211

Cover design: Unlikely Suburban Design
Text design: Mary Sanford

Library of Congress Cataloging-in-Publication Data
Smith, Shelley Ann, 1958–
    The fibromyalgia cookbook : more than 120 easy & delicious recipes /
Shelley Ann Smith ; foreword by Alison Bested and Alan C. Logan.
        p. cm.
Includes bibliographical references and index.
    ISBN 1-58182-270-7 (alk. paper)
    1. Fibromyalgia—Diet therapy—Recipes. I. Title.
    RC927.3 .S64 2002
    616.7'4—dc21

                                                            2002001699

Printed in the United States of America
    3 4 5 6 7—07 06 05 04 03

This book is dedicated to my parents, who have supported me through my many trials, and to my wonderful children, Stephen, Kristin, Adam, and Barrett. I would also like to thank my sisters, Lea, Robin, and Jennifer, for believing in me. To my special friend, Father Dominick, who has given me courage, faith, and hope.

Contents

Foreword

What Is Fibromyalgia?

Fibromyalgia (FM) is a chronic musculoskeletal disorder that is characterized by widespread pain and tenderness throughout the body. In accordance with the American College of Rheumatology guidelines, the diagnosis of FM is based on a history of chronic widespread pain and the finding of tender points by a physician (*Arthr Rheumatol,* 1990). Often the pain and tenderness are accompanied by multiple symptoms including fatigue, insomnia, memory and concentration difficulties and gastrointestinal (GI) complaints. Fibromyalgia is not a rare condition; in fact it is one of the most common rheumatic illnesses. The prevalence of FM among women is 3.4 percent or 3400 women per 100,000 and among men is 0.5 percent or 500 per 100,000. Clearly, FM is a major concern in the field of women's health.

Despite volumes of international research, the cause of FM remains unknown. Numerous studies have shown physiological disturbances among FM patients, including hormonal and neurotransmitter abnormalities. Not only are FM patients more sensitive to pain after illness onset, they are more sensitive in general—this can include previously tolerated material, odors, and even food. To date research has not revealed a fully effective treatment protocol for FM patients. There is evidence that low-dose anti-depressant medication and carefully monitored exercise programs are of benefit. Recently, investigators have suggested that a multidisciplinary, holistic treatment approach—one that emphasizes education and support—may be the most appropriate. Based on clinical observations and published literature, we believe that proper dietary choices can be a helpful component in FM treatment efforts.

How can dietary changes help?

Research has shown that almost half of all FM patients attempt dietary changes and many report this as a helpful approach. In the case of the related disorder of chronic fatigue syndrome (CFS), over 70 percent of those who attempt dietary changes report it as the most helpful complementary or alternative intervention. These dietary changes are, however, commonly attempted without guidance and support. Patients are often unaware of alternative choices and meal plans—this usually results in poor compliance beyond the short-term.

A number of research papers have shown that vegetarian and vegan diets, at least over the short-term, can be beneficial in the reduction of FM symptoms. In a study published in the *Scandinavian Journal of Rheumatology* (Kaartinen et al., 2000), FM patients on a vegan diet for three months had a 30 percent reduction in tender point numbers and an almost complete elimination of the need for painkillers. The increased intake of fruit and vegetable antioxidant and anti-inflammatory phytonutrients is thought to play a part in the benefit of such diets. This doesn't mean that FM patients should become vegetarian or vegan; however, it does suggest that reducing pro-inflammatory animal fat, particularly red meat, and increasing fruits and vegetables may indeed be beneficial.

Another area of recent research involves the elimination of food additives such as monosodium glutamate (MSG) and aspartame. In a series of case studies published in the *Annals of Pharmacotherapy* (Smith et al., 2001), the elimination of MSG and aspartame led to dramatic improvement in FM symptoms. The investigators reported worsening of symptoms when the patients were challenged with MSG and aspartame. It is possible that MSG, aspartame, and other chemical food additives gain access to the brain through a disturbed blood-brain barrier. Once inside the nervous system these chemicals can act as neurotoxins and disrupt normal transmission between nerve cells. Removal of dietary chemical additives has also shown symptom reduction in CFS. Investigators from the University of Newcastle, Australia, reported marked improvements in a number of symptoms, particularly those in the GI tract, when certain food chemicals including MSG were removed. These findings are very important considering that over 70 percent of FM and CFS patients meet the criteria for irritable bowel syndrome during the course of illness.

According to recent research published in the *Journal of the American College of Nutrition* (October 2001), food intolerances may play a role in the aggravation of FM symptoms. Food intolerances are negative bodily reactions caused by certain foods and are separate and distinct from the classic food allergy. In contrast to food allergy, where an immediate response is generally observed, the negative reaction to a food intolerance may be delayed and take a few days. While classic food allergy to foods such as peanuts and shellfish is quite rare in the adult population, food intolerances (also called food sensitivities) may be more frequent. Doctors often dismiss the symptoms aggravated by food intolerances, thinking them to be just "in the patient's head." In 2000, a very important paper published in the prestigious journal *Lancet* challenged this notion. It appears that when patients who are intolerant to foods are challenged with those foods they produce inflammatory cytokines that circulate in the blood. These cytokines can be responsible for the headaches, joint pain, and fatigue observed in FM and CFS.

While there are a number of methods to determine the existence of food intolerance, the elimination and challenge diet remains the gold standard. Suspect foods, for example dairy, wheat, citrus, and corn, are eliminated from the diet for a minimum of four days and a maximum of ten days. If symptoms clear at four days, then start the process at day five. If symptoms don't clear, continue until they do clear or until day ten if symptoms have not completely cleared. All of the suspect foods are left out of the diet at the same time. Symptoms may worsen on days two and three as the body goes through a withdrawal of the food. On the fifth day, if symptoms have cleared, one of the foods can be introduced back into the diet. A food diary needs to be kept to record a number of details. The suspected reactions, both physical and emotional, should be recorded before eliminating the suspected food items. The process of re-introducing the food is done one food at a time. This process should always be done the same way: in the morning, take your pulse for a full minute. Record this in the food diary. Eat a small quantity of the challenge food on an empty stomach (see *Testing of Common Problematic Foods* on the next page for sample quantities). Take your pulse again five, ten, and twenty minutes after eating the food. Record these in your food diary. Also in the food diary, record in separate columns any physical symptoms such as rash, heart palpitations, fatigue, or shortness of breath. In another column, record any emotional reactions, such as sleepiness, depression, stimulation, or anxiety. If your pulse rises by ten beats or more, or you have physical or emotional reactions, you may be having an adverse food reaction or a sensitivity reaction to the food in question. Stop the food challenge at that point. Score the severity of the reaction from zero to four. If symptoms occur, they will usually be those that you commonly experience, but they may be more severe than usual. To offset the symptoms, it is sometimes helpful to take one tablet of Alka Seltzer Gold (United States only) or to take 1 teaspoon of Bisalts (2 parts sodium bicarbonate to 1 part potassium bicarbonate—made by a pharmacist) in a glass of water. This may assist in clearing the reaction more quickly. Symptoms may occur within a few minutes or up to twenty-four hours after eating a food that is not tolerated. Do not test another food until the symptoms have cleared completely. If you do not react to the smallest sample of the food in question, then proceed to the larger portion sizes. The testing of various forms of the same food is also important and has been clinically developed by food allergy and intolerance expert Dr. Janice Joneja. Below are some suggestions.

TESTING OF COMMON PROBLEMATIC FOODS

WHEAT

TEST 1: Puffed wheat or cream of wheat
    (Sample portions: ¼ cup – ½ cup – 1 cup)
TEST 2: Yeast-free cracker
    (Sample portions: 2 – 4 – 8 crackers)
TEST 3: Regular bread
    (Sample portions: ½ slice – 1 slice – 2 slices)

CORN

Kernel corn
> (Sample portions: $1/4$ cup – $1/2$ cup – 1 cup)

MILK AND MILK PRODUCTS
(Each protein component needs to be tested individually)

TEST 1: Casein protein—white cheese (e.g., mozzarella, swiss)
> (Sample portions: 1 ounce – 2 ounces – 4 ounces)

TEST 2: Casein, Annatto (natural beta-carotene dye and biogenic amines—yellow/orange cheese (e.g., old cheddar)
> (Sample portions: 1 ounce – 2 ounces – 4 ounces)

TEST 3: Casein and whey proteins, e.g., lactaid milk
> (Sample portions: $1/4$ cup – $1/2$ cup – 1 cup)

TEST 4: Casein, whey, and lactose, e.g., regular milk
> (Sample portions: $1/4$ cup – $1/2$ cup – 1 cup)

TEST 5: Casein and modified milk, e.g., yogurt
> (Sample portions: $1/4$ cup – $1/2$ cup – 1 cup)

EGGS

TEST 1: Egg yolk
> (Sample portions: $1/2$ yolk – 1 yolk – 2 yolks)

TEST 2: Egg white
> (Sample portions: white only of $1/2$ – 1 – 2 cooked eggs)

• • •

This is a short elimination diet. More elaborate versions do exist. We recommend performing any elimination and challenge diet under the supervision of a nutritionally oriented doctor or a dietician. At no time should foods with previous history of a severe anaphylactic or asthmatic reaction be tested unless specifically ordered by your doctor in a setting equipped to deal with these problems

As clinicians we have seen the value of "food as medicine" in many of our patients. Research will undoubtedly continue to uncover the multiple benefits of complex phytonutrients found in fruits, vegetables, and other healthy foods. At the same time, it is hoped that research will shed more light on the reasons why certain foods provoke symptoms in some individuals and why certain chemicals, generally considered safe, may cause a worsening of symptoms among patients with FM and CFS.

In *The Fibromyalgia Cookbook,* Shelley Ann Smith has provided the instrument needed to increase compliance among those attempting dietary changes. She has provided options and alternatives, and most importantly she has given the FM patient/caretaker a variety of foods to choose from. One of the realistic concerns of clinicians related to dietary modifications is that if choices are too narrow and limiting, potential nutritional deficiencies could occur. FM patients need to eat a nutritionally balanced diet with adequate protein, fats, and carbohydrates based on individual caloric needs. This recipe book is not based on a restrictive diet but rather one that is inclusive of many healthy foods. As an FM patient herself, Ms. Smith provides a unique perspective on the dietary choices that have helped her in recovery efforts. She recognized a need for support and has filled the void well, hopefully making the lives of fellow sufferers a little easier. *The Fibromyalgia Cookbook* can be used, along with professional medical guidance, as a means to maintain a healthy diet, one that is so desperately needed when living with a chronic illness.

Enjoy,

Alison C. Bested, M.D., F.R.C.P.S.
Haematological Pathologist
Toronto, Canada

Alan C. Logan, N.D.
Doctor of Naturopathic Medicine
Clinical Consultant
Toronto, Canada

References

1. Millea, P. J., Holloway, R. L. Treating fibromyalgia. *Am Fam Physician* 2000; 62:1575–82.

2. Littlejohn, G. Fibromyalgia: What is it and how do we treat it? *Aust Fam Physician* 2001; 30:327–33.

3. Emms, T. M., et al. Food intolerance in chronic fatigue syndrome. Abstract #15 presented at the proceedings of the American Association for Chronic Fatigue Syndrome. January 2001. Seattle, Washington.

4. Pioro-Boisset, M., Esdaile, J. M., Fitzcharles, M. Alternative medicine use in fibromyalgia syndrome. *Arthr Care Res* 1996; 9:13–17.

5. Nisenbaum, R., Reyes, M., Jones, A., Reeves, W. C. Course of illness among patients with chronic fatigue syndrome in Wichita, Kansas. Abstract #49 presented at the proceedings of the American Association for Chronic Fatigue Syndrome conference, January 2001. Seattle, WA.

6. Lukaczer, D., Schiltz, B., Liska, D. J. A pilot trial evaluating the effect of an inflammatory-modulating medical food in patients with fibromyalgia. *Clin Pract Altern Med* 2000; 1(3):148–156.

7. Kaartinen, K., Lammi, K., Hypen, M., Nenonen, M., Hanninen, O., Rauma, A. L. Vegan diet alleviates fibromyalgia symptoms. *Scand J Rheumatol* 2000; 29:308–313.

8. Hostmark, A. T., Lystad, E., Vellar, O. D., Hovi, K., Berg, J. E. Reduced plasma fibrinogen, serum peroxides, lipids, and apolipoproteins after a 3-week vegetarian diet. *Plant Foods Hum Nutr* 1993; 43:55–61.

9. Haugen, M., Kjeldsen-Kragh, J., Nordvag, B. Y., Forre, O. Diet and disease symptoms in rheumatic diseases—results of a question-naire based survey. *Clin Rheumatol* 1991; 10:401–407.

10. Hanninen, O., Kaartinen, K., Rauma, A. L., Nenonen, M., Torronen, R., Hakkinen, S., et al. Antioxidants in vegan diet and rheumatic disorders. *Toxicology* 2000; 155:45–53.

11. Smith, J. D., Terpening, C. M., Schmidt, S., Gums, J. G. Relief of fibromyalgia symptoms following discontinuation of dietary excito-toxins. *Ann Pharmacother* 2001; 35:702–706.

12. Jacobsen, M. B., et al. Relation between food provocation and systemic immune activation in patients with food intolerance. *Lancet* 2000; 356(9227):400–401

13. Edman, J. S., et al. A pilot study of elimination/challenge diets in patients with fibromyalgia (FM). *J Am Coll Nutr* 2001; 19(5):574

14. Wolfe, F., et al. The American College of Rheumatology 1990 Criteria for the Classification of Fibromyalgia: Report of the Mulicenter Criteria Committee. *Arthr Rheumatol* 1990; 33:160–72.

15. Joneja, J. V. *Dietary Management of Food Allergies and Intolerances. A Comprehensive Guide.* 2nd edition. J. A. Hall Pub. Vancouver, Canada. 1998.

The Fibromyalgia Cookbook

Introduction

On December 5, 1995, my life was radically changed in many unimaginable ways when my youngest son and I were involved in a head-on car accident. We both survived the wreck and the seemingly harmless surface wounds soon disappeared. Even the nightmares abated after a while. However, my body was shaken to the very marrow of my bones, leaving my defenses at an all-time low, and I became ill with the painful condition called Fibromyalgia.

"Fibro" inflicts terrible wounds that leave no scars, and so it is very difficult to explain and much more difficult to treat. Many months went by visiting doctors for their diagnosis, and the confusion surrounding my problem intensified. Before long it was evident that I would need to alter the very way I live. My career, my lifestyle, my motivations, even my daily tasks and routines all came together for readjustment in a very sobering way. Much courage and trust was needed.

My work experience before the accident included a job as a pharmacy technician. I was well aware of the many drugs available, the pain suppressants, and the myriad of pharmaceuticals. However, my curiosity led me to delve into the natural side of things. I explored the healthy food alternative, herbs and natural foods. I became more aware of the benefits of God's own medicine.

All this knowledge really became beneficial after the accident. Those natural foods and herbs actually helped me, gave me new energy, and I continued to explore the possibilities. I discovered the old saying "You are what you eat" is poignantly relevant to people suffering with Fibro. Their very fabric and fiber are so sensitive and under continual test that any food substances put into their bodies can have intense effects. The solution? Pure foods with no additives, the least toxins, and the most nutrition.

Eating the right foods with Fibro is not that difficult. You need only to remember a few things and follow a few basic rules. No red meat is easy to remember. And did you know that green peppers contain a compound called *solanine,* which affects enzyme function in the muscles causing pain? That ginger is a powerful antioxidant? We don't eat eggplant and we stay away from heavy, starchy foods because they are hard to tolerate. Our diets are low in sodium, low in fat, with no sugar. But don't worry, sugar lovers, because there are natural sweet foods we can enjoy like honey and fruit! We use spelt flour instead of white flour. We love rice pasta and soya butter. We eat extra virgin olive oil and flaxseed oil for salads. There are countless possibilities to satisfy every want.

I hope you enjoy the ideas I have compiled in this recipe book. I know that all my trusty taste testers—my loving family—have enjoyed helping me.

I want to thank my tasting crew and my family and God for giving me the strength and determination to help me help myself feel better through the ways in which I've altered my life. To the friend of my heart, who with the greatest compassion in my Fibro needs and tender love has given me much consolation and support, I say a big thank you!

Glossary

Water helps with muscle movement, skin tone, digestion, brain function, hair growth and a whole host of other functions that keep us alive. Filtered, distilled water is your best bet, and the more, the better. Drink at least eight 8oz glasses of fresh clean water every day. Drinking so much water may be hard for some people. Try adding a slice of lemon or lime into your water for a refreshing taste. Mint leaves or a slice of orange is also very nice. Remember it is imperative for fibromyalgia sufferers to drink lots of water!

Spelt Flour is more than just a nutritious product. The whole grain flour is the answer for those people who want to eat good, tasty whole grain products. Spelt is organic, unbleached and is the grain with most of the bran removed, and nothing added. Spelt contains special carbohydrates, which stimulate the body's immune system. One of the most beneficial differences between spelt and wheat is the fact that many wheat and gluten-sensitive individuals have been able to include spelt-based foods in their diets. It's higher in B-vitamins and fiber than ordinary bread wheats and has larger amounts of both simple and complex carbohydrates, proteins and several amino acids.

White Flour invokes an inflammatory response in the body and this causes pain.

Red Bell Peppers are a better anticancer choice than green peppers because they contain added carotenes. Red bell peppers also supply powerful antioxidant properties. Green peppers contain a compound called solanine that affects enzyme function in the muscles, and this causes pain.

Ginger, Rosemary, Pepper, Oregano, and **Thyme** are powerful antioxidants.

Brown Rice is high in fiber and can possibly help to lower cholesterol. Brown rice is very high in vitamin B-6 and magnesium. It provides thiamin (which is vital to nerve function), niacin, copper, and zinc. Research studies indicate that vitamin E from brown rice tends to strengthen the immune system and reduce the risk of heart disease and cataracts.

Soya Protein is an easy, inexpensive, and healthful alternative to meat. Soya products are dairy-free and do not contain saturated fat.

Unprocessed Food: Eat as much as possible!

Caffeine and Sugar: Avoid them!

Low-Fat Dairy Products: Use them!

Red Meat: Limit or eliminate!

Soups

Cauliflower Soup

6	cups water
1	head of cauliflower, cut in small pieces
1	medium onion, finely chopped
3	tablespoons soya butter
1	clove garlic
¼	teaspoon pepper
¼	cup low-sodium chicken stock
¼	cup spelt flour
1	cup skim milk

In a large pot add 6 cups of water, the cauliflower, onion, butter, garlic, pepper, and chicken stock. Bring to a boil. Reduce the heat and simmer until the cauliflower is tender.

In a blender purée the soup, working in batches if necessary. Return the soup to the pot.

In a medium jar combine the flour and milk. Shake until smooth. Add the flour mixture to the soup and cook over medium heat, stirring constantly, until the soup thickens.

Bring to a boil and serve.

MAKES 6 SERVINGS

Chilled Cucumber Soup

2	**cups chopped seeded cucumber**
1	**cup low-sodium chicken broth**
½	**cup low-fat yogurt**
1	**teaspoon lemon juice**
¼	**teaspoon Tabasco sauce**
½	**cup low-fat cottage cheese**

In a blender combine all of the ingredients and blend until smooth. Chill.

Serve in cold soup dishes with slivered cucumbers and fresh ground pepper for garnish.

MAKES 4 SERVINGS

Creamed Carrot Soup

2	tablespoons extra virgin olive oil
1	onion, finely chopped
10	medium carrots, chopped
¼	cup spelt flour
3	cups low-sodium chicken stock
1	bay leaf
3	tablespoons chopped fresh coriander
2	cups skim milk
	Fresh ground pepper

In a saucepan heat the olive oil over medium heat and sauté the onion until tender. Add the carrots and cook for 15 minutes.

Sprinkle the flour over the carrot mixture and stir until well blended. Slowly pour the stock into the saucepan, stirring until smooth. Add the bay leaf and coriander, and cook for 20 minutes.

Remove and discard the bay leaf.

In a blender purée the soup, working in batches if necessary. Return the soup to the saucepan. Stir in the milk and pepper. Cook over low heat until the soup reaches the desired temperature.

MAKES 6 TO 8 SERVINGS

Crabby Clam Soup

1	14-ounce can Italian stewed tomatoes
$\frac{1}{2}$	cup grated carrots
1	cup finely chopped celery
1	cup finely chopped onion
1	clove garlic, minced
	Fresh ground pepper
1	small tin crab meat with juice
1	10-ounce can clams with juice
2	cups skim milk
3	cups water
$\frac{1}{2}$	cup spelt flour mixed with $\frac{1}{2}$ cup water
2	tablespoons low-sodium chicken bouillon powder

In a large saucepan combine the tomatoes, carrots, celery, onion, garlic, and pepper. Cook over medium heat until tender.

Add the crab meat and clams with their juices, the skim milk, and the 3 cups of water. In a medium bowl mix the flour and $\frac{1}{2}$ cup water with the chicken bouillon until smooth. Add to the saucepan and cook, stirring often, until boiling and thickened. Season with pepper to taste. Serve.

MAKES 6 SERVINGS

Mushroom Chowder

¼	**cup soya butter**
1	**medium onion, finely chopped**
2	**pounds fresh mushrooms, chopped**
½	**cup spelt flour**
4	**cups low-sodium chicken stock**

In a soup pot melt the butter over medium heat and sauté the onions until soft. Add the mushrooms and cook for 30 minutes.

Blend in the spelt flour. Slowly add the chicken stock, stirring until smooth. Cover and simmer for 30 minutes.

In a blender purée the soup, working in batches if necessary. Return the soup to the pot and reheat if necessary.

If desired add a dollop of fat-free sour cream to each serving.

MAKES 6 SERVINGS

Lentil Soup

1	cup split red lentils
3	tablespoons soya butter
1	medium onion, finely chopped
2	stalks celery, finely chopped
2	carrots, finely chopped
	Grated rind of 1 lemon
4	cups low-sodium vegetable stock
	Fresh ground pepper

Rinse and sort the lentils, removing any stones.

In a stock pot melt the butter over medium heat and sauté the onion until transparent. Add the celery and carrots, and cook for 5 minutes.

Stir in the lentils. Add the lemon rind, vegetable stock, and pepper. Bring the soup to a boil. Reduce the heat and simmer for 20 minutes.

In a blender process the soup briefly, leaving some texture. Return the soup to the pot and reheat if necessary.

MAKES 4 SERVINGS

Split Pea Soup

8	cups water
2	cups dried split peas
4	tablespoons low-sodium chicken stock
1	medium onion, finely chopped
1	medium carrot, diced
1	stalk of celery, finely chopped
1	tablespoon minced fresh dill
2	tablespoons low-sodium soya sauce

In a large stock pot place the water and peas and bring to a boil. Reduce the heat and simmer for 30 minutes.

In a large skillet cook the onions, carrots, celery, and dill in the chicken stock until tender.

Drain the peas, reserving the liquid. Add the peas to the skillet with the vegetables and cook for 5 minutes over low heat. Transfer the mixture to the soup pot and add the reserved liquid and the soya sauce. Simmer for 30 minutes.

In a blender purée the soup, working in batches if necessary. Return the soup to the pot and reheat if necessary.

MAKES 6 TO 8 SERVINGS

Zucchini Soup

2	green onions, finely chopped
4	tablespoons low-sodium chicken stock
2	cups shredded zucchini
3	cups skim milk
4	tablespoons finely chopped fresh parsley
1	teaspoon dried thyme
½	teaspoon ground coriander

In a large saucepan cook the onions in the stock for 4 minutes. Add the zucchini and cook for 5 minutes or until tender. Add the parsley, thyme, coriander, and milk, and bring to a boil. Reduce the heat and simmer for 30 minutes.

In a blender purée the soup, working in batches if necessary. Return to the pan and reheat before serving.

MAKES 4 SERVINGS

Turkey Bean Soup

2	cups low-sodium chicken stock
1	cup thinly sliced celery
1	cup thinly sliced carrots
$\frac{1}{2}$	cup finely chopped onion
$\frac{1}{2}$	teaspoon ground thyme
$\frac{1}{4}$	teaspoon dried basil leaves
	Fresh ground pepper
2	garlic cloves, minced
1	bay leaf
$1\frac{1}{2}$	cups cubed cooked turkey
3	cups tomato juice
1	can cannellini beans, drained and rinsed

In a large saucepan combine the chicken stock, vegetables, thyme, basil, pepper, garlic, and bay leaf. Bring to a boil. Reduce the heat and simmer for 15 minutes. Add the remaining ingredients and simmer until heated.

MAKES 4 SERVINGS

Tomato Chick Pea Soup

1	**cup dried chick peas**
3	**tablespoons extra virgin olive oil**
2	**garlic cloves**
1½	**cups chopped tomatoes**
3	**cups water**
1	**teaspoon dried basil**
1	**chicken bouillon cube**
	Fresh ground pepper
1	**cup small rice pasta**

In a stock pot cover the peas with water and soak overnight. Drain and discard the water. Place the peas in a large pan and cover with water. Bring to a boil. Reduce the heat, cover, and simmer for 1 hour until the peas are tender.

In a skillet heat the oil and sauté the garlic cloves. When browned, remove and discard the garlic. Add the tomatoes and their juice, water, and basil, and simmer for 20 minutes.

Add the drained peas, bouillon cube, and pepper. Stir well and simmer for 10 minutes.

Bring to a boil, add the pasta, and cook for 10 minutes.

MAKES 6 SERVINGS

Sweet Potato Soup

¼	cup extra virgin olive oil
3	cloves garlic, minced
2	medium onions, diced
2	teaspoons thyme
3	bay leaves
10	cups low-sodium vegetable stock
1	cup lentils
2	stalks celery, finely chopped
1	large carrot, finely chopped
½	cup finely chopped fresh parsley
2	medium sweet potatoes, peeled and diced
	Fresh ground pepper

In a large stockpot heat the olive oil over medium heat. Add the garlic, onions, thyme, and bay leaves, and sauté for 10 minutes.

Stir in the vegetable stock, lentils, celery, carrot, and parsley. Bring to a boil. Reduce the heat and simmer uncovered for 40 minutes.

Add the sweet potatoes and cook for 20 minutes. Discard the bay leaves. Season with pepper. Remove 3 cups of the soup and purée in a blender, and return to the pot.

MAKES 4 TO 6 SERVINGS

Cream of Chicken Soup

4	tablespoons soya butter
8	shallots, thinly sliced
2	medium carrots, thinly sliced
3	stalks celery, thinly sliced
3	boneless, skinless, chicken breasts, finely chopped
¼	cup spelt flour
5	cups low-sodium chicken stock
	Fresh ground pepper
¾	cup light cream

In a large saucepan melt the butter over medium-low heat and add the shallots, carrots, celery, and chicken. Cook gently for 10 minutes.

Stir in the flour, blending well. Slowly add the chicken stock, stirring constantly, until smooth. Season with pepper. Cook over low heat for 15 minutes.

Blend in the light cream. Serve.

MAKES 6 SERVINGS

Salads

Beet and Apple Salad

1	*large beet, cooked and grated*
1	*large beet, raw and grated*
2	*green apples, thinly sliced*

DRESSING

2	*tablespoons lemon juice*
4	*tablespoons extra virgin olive oil*
1	*tablespoon finely chopped fresh dill*
	Fresh ground pepper

In a salad bowl combine the beets and apples.

In a jar combine the lemon juice, oil, dill, and pepper. Shake well. Pour over the beets and apples.

MAKES 4 SERVINGS

Crab Rice Salad

1	can crab, drained
1½	cups cooked basmati brown rice
¼	cup finely chopped celery
½	teaspoon finely chopped fresh parsley
¼	cup sliced olives
2½	tablespoons low-fat mayonnaise
	Lettuce

In a salad bowl combine the first six ingredients. Mix together, adding more mayonnaise if needed.

Serve over lettuce.

MAKES 4 SERVINGS

Mushroom Salad

½	cup extra virgin olive oil
3	tablespoons lemon juice
1	tablespoon white wine vinegar
1	clove garlic, crushed
¼	teaspoon chili powder
1	pound fresh mushrooms, thinly sliced
1	tablespoon finely chopped fresh chives
1	tablespoon finely chopped fresh parsley
½	red bell pepper, diced

In a jar combine the olive oil, lemon juice, vinegar, garlic, and chili powder. Shake and pour over the mushrooms. Toss and leave for 3 hours.

Gently stir in the chives, parsley, and red pepper. Serve.

MAKES 6 SERVINGS

Chicken and Shrimp Salad

1	cup cubed cooked chicken
1	cup small cooked shrimp
½	cup chopped celery
½	cup chopped red bell pepper
½	cup chopped green onion
½	cup low-fat mayonnaise
1	tablespoon horseradish
1	teaspoon dill weed
	Fresh ground pepper
5	cups shredded iceberg lettuce

In a medium bowl combine the chicken, shrimp, celery, pepper, and onion.

In a small bowl mix together the mayonnaise, horseradish, dill weed, and pepper. Add to the shrimp mixture and stir well. Chill for 30 minutes.

Place the lettuce on 4 plates and spoon the salad on top.

MAKES 4 TO 6 SERVINGS

Chicken Salad with Cashews

6	boneless chicken breasts, poached and shredded
3	celery stalks, cut into thin strips
1	large red bell pepper, cut into thin strips
3	green onions, sliced
$\frac{1}{2}$	cup cashews
3	cups shredded romaine lettuce

MUSTARD DRESSING

1	egg
$\frac{1}{4}$	cup fresh orange juice
$\frac{1}{4}$	cup extra virgin olive oil
$1\frac{1}{2}$	teaspoons red wine vinegar
$1\frac{1}{2}$	teaspoons Dijon mustard
$\frac{1}{2}$	teaspoon honey
$\frac{1}{2}$	cup fresh parsley, chopped
	Fresh ground pepper

In a large bowl combine the chicken, celery, red pepper, onions, and cashews.

In a blender combine the dressing ingredients. Blend well.

Add $\frac{1}{2}$ cup dressing to the salad and toss to coat. Serve over lettuce.

MAKES 6 LARGE SERVINGS

Chicken and Tangerine Salad

3	chicken breasts, boneless and skinless
4	tangerines, peeled and sectioned
3	tablespoons chopped pecans
3	chives, finely chopped
1	tablespoon extra virgin olive oil
2	tablespoons fresh orange juice

Preheat the oven to 350°.

Place the chicken in a baking dish. Bake for 1 hour.

Cool and shred into bite-size pieces. Place in a medium bowl and add the tangerine sections, pecans, and chives.

In a small bowl mix together the olive oil and orange juice. Pour over the salad and toss until coated. Serve at room temperature.

MAKES 4 SERVINGS

Raw Carrot and Green Apple Salad

2	**green apples, cored and grated**
	Juice from 1 lemon
2	**medium carrots, grated**

DRESSING

4	**tablespoons extra virgin olive oil**
4	**tablespoons balsamic vinegar**

In a salad bowl toss the apples in lemon juice. Mix in the carrots.

In a jar mix the oil and vinegar together. Pour over the salad and blend.

MAKES 4 SERVINGS

Carrot and Raisin Slaw

6	medium carrots
3/4	cup diced celery
1/2	cup raisins
1/4	cup diced onion
1/2	cup diced apple
1/2	cup low-fat mayonnaise
	Fresh ground pepper

Clean and grate the carrots.

In a medium bowl combine the carrots, celery, onion, raisins, and apple. Mix in the mayonnaise and season with pepper. Chill.

MAKES 6 SERVINGS

Carrot Salad with Honey Mustard Dressing

1	**large leek**
2	**tablespoons extra virgin olive oil**
6	**carrots, finely julienned**
1	**red bell pepper, seeded and cut into thin strips**

DRESSING

2	**tablespoons red wine vinegar**
2	**tablespoons extra virgin olive oil**
2	**teaspoons Dijon mustard**
1	**teaspoon honey**

Leave 1 inch of green top on the leek and trim off the end. Cut into 2-inch slivers.

In large skillet heat the oil over medium heat. Add the leeks and sauté for 3 minutes.

Add the carrot and red pepper. Cover and cook until tender crisp.

To prepare the dressing, in a small bowl whisk together red wine vinegar, oil, mustard, and honey. Stir the dressing into the vegetables. Chill for 3 hours before serving.

MAKES 4 SERVINGS

Fresh Citrus Mint Salad

3	large oranges
2	white or pink grapefruits
8	sprigs mint

Peel the oranges and grapefruits. Separate the sections of fruit. Squeeze the membranes to extract all the juice into a small bowl.

Arrange the segments in a bowl. Chop the mint very finely and stir into the fruit juice. Spoon the juice over the fruit segments and chill.

MAKES 4 SERVINGS

Chicken Waldorf Salad

¾	cup low-fat mayonnaise
2	tablespoons skim milk
2	cups diced apple
2	cups diced cooked chicken
¾	cup diced celery
½	cup chopped walnuts
½	cup raisins
2	cups shredded lettuce

In a medium bowl mix the mayonnaise and milk together. Add the apple and mix. Stir in the chicken pieces, celery, walnuts, and raisins. Blend well together. Spoon the salad over the lettuce leaves.

MAKES 4 SERVINGS

Pink Grapefruit and Scallop Salad

¾	**cup scallops**
2	**pink grapefruits, sectioned**
1	**tablespoon minced chives**
2	**tablespoons grapefruit juice**
1	**tablespoon extra virgin olive oil**
½	**teaspoon Dijon mustard**
	Lettuce leaves

Cut the scallops in half. In boiling water cook the scallops for 2 to 3 minutes.

In a salad bowl combine the grapefruit sections and chives. Add the scallops.

In a small bowl whisk together the grapefruit juice, oil, and mustard. Pour over the scallop mixture and toss well to combine. Serve chilled on lettuce leaves.

MAKES 4 SERVINGS

Jen's Rice and Black Bean Salad

1	cup uncooked basmati brown rice
	Low-sodium chicken stock
1	14-ounce can black beans
1	large tomato, seeded and chopped
1	bunch fresh cilantro, finely chopped
3	green onions, chopped
	Juice and grated peel of 2 limes
$^1/_2$	cup extra virgin olive oil

Cook the rice in low-sodium chicken stock according to the package directions and let cool.

Rinse the black beans and add to the rice. Add the tomato, chopped cilantro, and green onions.

In a small bowl combine the lime juice, peel, and olive oil, and mix well. Pour over the rice mixture and stir well. Chill before serving.

MAKES 8 SERVINGS

Pasta Tuna Salad

1½ cups brown rice shell pasta
1   8-ounce can red kidney beans, drained
1   cup chopped fresh mushrooms
1   14-ounce can flaked white tuna, packed
     in water
¼   cup chopped fresh chives
1   tablespoon dried oregano

DRESSING
½   cup extra virgin olive oil
3   tablespoons white wine vinegar
     Juice of one lemon
1   tablespoon Dijon mustard
     Fresh ground pepper

Cook the pasta shells according to the package directions. Drain and rinse.

In a small bowl mix the dressing ingredients together.

In a large bowl mix the pasta, beans, mushrooms, tuna, chives, and oregano. Pour the dressing over the salad and toss to coat. Chill for 1 hour before serving.

MAKES 4 SERVINGS

Pineapple Chicken Salad

2	cups diced cooked chicken
5	slices fresh pineapple, diced
1	banana, sliced
³⁄₄	cup chopped celery
¹⁄₂	cup low-fat mayonnaise
2	tablespoons lemon juice
	Salad greens

In a large bowl toss all ingredients together except the salad greens. Line salad bowls with greens and spoon the chicken mixture on top.

MAKES 6 SERVINGS

Zucchini Salad

2	cups thinly sliced zucchini
4	radishes, julienned
1	green onion, chopped

DRESSING

6	tablespoons low-fat mayonnaise
5	teaspoons skim milk
½	teaspoon garlic powder

In a salad bowl toss the zucchini, radishes, and onion together.

In a small bowl mix the mayonnaise, skim milk, and garlic powder together. Pour over salad and toss.

MAKES 4 SERVINGS

Salmon Seashell Pasta Salad

1	can red salmon, drained
1	cup small rice pasta seashells
1	medium red bell pepper, cut into slices
½	cup thinly sliced celery
½	cup diced red onion
¾	cup low-fat mayonnaise
1	tablespoon white wine vinegar
2	tablespoons dried dill

Break the salmon into chunks and set aside.

In a large pot cook the pasta until tender. Drain well.

In a large bowl combine the pasta, salmon, red pepper, celery, and red onion.

In a small bowl whisk together the mayonnaise, vinegar, and dill. Pour the dressing over the salad and toss to combine.

MAKES 4 SERVINGS

Curry Bean Salad

1	teaspoon ground cumin
2	teaspoons curry powder
1	14-ounce can kidney beans, drained
1	red onion, diced
2	tomatoes, chopped
2	stalks celery, chopped
2	green onions, sliced
2	tablespoons lime juice
1	tablespoon extra virgin olive oil
¼	cup fresh chopped coriander

In a small skillet heat the cumin and curry powder and set aside.

Place the kidney beans in a large bowl. Add the onion, tomatoes, celery, and green onions.

In a small bowl mix the lime juice, olive oil, cumin, and curry powder. Pour over the bean mixture. Stir in the coriander. Cover and chill, stirring occasionally.

MAKES 4 SERVINGS

Vegetable Turkey Salad

2	cups fresh broccoli florets
3	cups diced cooked turkey
1	medium red bell pepper, coarsely chopped
1	cup fat-free sour cream
3	tablespoons low-fat mayonnaise
1	tablespoon white wine vinegar
1	tablespoon dried basil
1	clove garlic, minced
	Fresh ground pepper

Cook the broccoli until bright green and tender crisp. Drain and rinse.

In a salad bowl place the turkey, broccoli, and bell pepper.

In a small bowl whisk the sour cream, mayonnaise, vinegar, basil, garlic, and pepper together. Pour the dressing over the turkey and vegetables. Toss to gently coat.

MAKES 4 TO 6 SERVINGS

Fresh Fruit Salad

¼	honeydew melon, cut into bite-size pieces
¼	cantaloupe, cut into bite-size pieces
2	peaches, sliced
1	banana, cubed
2	tablespoons honey
½	teaspoon fresh lemon juice

In a medium bowl combine the fruit. In a small bowl blend the honey and lemon juice. Drizzle over the fruit.

MAKES 4 SERVINGS

Spinach Salad

4	**cups torn fresh spinach**
½	**cup cubed red bell pepper**
½	**cup thinly sliced red onion, separated into rings**
	Favorite salad dressing
¼	**cup sunflower seeds**

In a salad bowl combine the spinach, red pepper, and onion rings together.

Pour on dressing and mix. Sprinkle with sunflower seeds.

MAKES 4 SERVINGS

Tomato and Sweet Pepper Salad

3	red bell peppers
5	tomatoes, peeled and seeded
1	cup sliced cucumber
1	clove garlic, minced
	Fresh ground pepper
1	tablespoon extra virgin olive oil
1	tablespoon wine vinegar
2	tablespoons chopped fresh coriander

On a greased grill, cook the peppers over medium heat, turning often, for 20 minutes.

Peel off the skin from the peppers. Core, seed, and cut lengthwise into 1-inch strips.

Cut the tomatoes into thin wedges.

In a salad bowl, combine the peppers, tomatoes, cucumber, garlic, and pepper. Drizzle with olive oil and vinegar, and toss. Add coriander and toss. Let stand for 1 hour.

MAKES 4 SERVINGS

Tossed Salad with Sunflower Seeds

1	**head of iceberg lettuce**
4	**tomatoes, chopped**
½	**pound fresh mushrooms**
1	**cup fresh bean sprouts**
½	**cup sunflower seeds**
	Favorite salad dressing

In a salad bowl toss all salad ingredients together and serve with salad dressing.

MAKES 6 SERVINGS

Strawberry Banana Salad

½	**cup sliced fresh strawberries**
½	**cup sliced bananas**
½	**cup low-fat cottage cheese**
2	**tablespoons plain low-fat yogurt**
2	**tablespoons chopped walnuts**
4	**romaine lettuce leaves, torn into bite-size pieces**

In a small bowl combine the fruit, cottage cheese, yogurt, and walnuts.

Arrange the lettuce in a serving bowl and top with the fruit mixture.

MAKES 1 SERVING

Curry Salad

2	tins shrimp
2	cups finely chopped celery
1	10-ounce can water chestnuts, sliced
1	cup fresh bean sprouts
2	green onions, chopped
1/4	cup low-fat mayonnaise
1/4	teaspoon curry powder

Drain and rinse the shrimp. Transfer to a salad bowl. Add the celery, water chestnuts, bean sprouts, and onions.

In a small bowl mix the mayonnaise and curry powder together. Spoon over the shrimp mixture. Toss to coat.

MAKES 4 SERVINGS

Veggies

Balsamic Carrots

5	small carrots, sliced diagonally
2	tablespoons balsamic vinegar
2	teaspoons honey
1	teaspoon extra virgin olive oil
$1/2$	teaspoon Dijon mustard
1	teaspoon dried basil
	Fresh ground pepper

In a large saucepan with 1 cup of water, add the carrots and bring to a boil. Cover, reduce the heat, and simmer for 10 minutes. Drain the carrots and return to the saucepan.

In a small bowl combine the vinegar and remaining five ingredients, stirring well with a wire whisk.

Add to the carrots, and cook over medium heat for 5 minutes, stirring often.

MAKES 4 SERVINGS

Parmesan Sautéed Zucchini

2	tablespoons extra virgin olive oil
2	cloves garlic, minced
2	medium size zucchini, cut into thick slices
	Fresh ground pepper
	Parmesan cheese

In a skillet heat the oil over medium heat and sauté the garlic for 2 minutes.

Add the zucchini and cook over medium heat until tender. Season with pepper. Sprinkle with Parmesan cheese.

MAKES 4 SERVINGS

Sesame Green Beans

1	pound green beans
2	tablespoons sesame seeds
1	tablespoon rice wine
2	teaspoons low-sodium soya sauce
1	teaspoon sesame oil
	Fresh ground pepper

Trim the green beans. In a large pot of boiling water, cook the beans for 5 minutes or until tender. Drain.

In a small skillet toast the sesame seeds over medium-high heat, stirring often, until golden.

In a small bowl combine the rice wine, low-sodium soya sauce, and sesame oil. Toss with the beans. Add pepper to taste. Sprinkle with sesame seeds.

MAKES 4 SERVINGS

Stir-Fried Squash

1	tablespoon extra virgin olive oil
1	clove garlic, crushed
1	teaspoon curry powder
1	teaspoon fresh grated ginger
1	onion, sliced
1	winter squash, cut into large chunks
2	tablespoons coriander
1	teaspoon low-sodium soya sauce
	Fresh ground pepper

In a skillet or wok heat the oil and stir-fry the garlic, curry powder, ginger, and onion for 2 minutes.

Add the squash and cook for 5 minutes more.

Toss with the coriander and soya sauce. Serve immediately.

MAKES 4 SERVINGS

Sesame Zucchini and Broccoli in Ginger

1	tablespoon extra virgin olive oil
½	head broccoli, cut into florets
1	medium size zucchini, cut into slices
	Fresh ground pepper

SAUCE

1	tablespoon low-sodium soya sauce
1	tablespoon grated fresh ginger
1	tablespoon sesame seeds
2	teaspoons cornstarch, blended with ½ cup low-sodium vegetable stock

In a large skillet or wok heat the oil and stir-fry the broccoli and zucchini for 2 to 3 minutes.

In a small bowl combine the soya, ginger, sesame seeds, and cornstarch mixture. Pour over the vegetables and cook for 3 minutes or until the sauce thickens. Season with pepper.

MAKES 4 SERVINGS

Dilled Mushrooms in Sour Cream

1	**pound fresh mushrooms, quartered**
3	**tablespoons soya butter**
5	**green onions, thinly sliced**
2	**tablespoons spelt flour**
1	**tablespoon fresh squeezed lemon juice**
2	**tablespoons chopped fresh dill**
	Fresh ground pepper
¾	**cup non-fat sour cream**
	Paprika

Clean the mushrooms and pat dry.

In a large skillet melt the soya butter and sauté the mushrooms and onions for 1 minute. Blend in the flour. Add the lemon juice, dill, and pepper. Stir in the sour cream. Heat through. Sprinkle with paprika.

MAKES 4 SERVINGS

Curry Glazed Carrots

12	*medium size carrots*
2	*tablespoons soya butter*
1	*clove garlic, minced*
1	*tablespoon chopped fresh gingerroot*
1½	*teaspoons curry powder*
1½	*cups low-sodium chicken stock*
2	*tablespoons honey*

Peel and cut the carrots into thick slices.

In a skillet, heat the soya butter and sauté the garlic and ginger over medium heat for 1 minute. Add the curry powder and cook 1 minute.

Add the carrots, stock, and honey, and cook, stirring occasionally, until the liquid evaporates.

MAKES 4 TO 6 SERVINGS

Lemon Parsley Turnips

1	medium turnip, cut into small cubes
2	tablespoons soya butter
1	green onion, sliced
2	tablespoons chopped fresh parsley
2	teaspoons lemon juice

In a medium pot cook the turnip in boiling water for 15 minutes. Drain.

Stir in the butter, onion, parsley, and lemon juice. Serve.

MAKES 4 SERVINGS

Asparagus and Cashew Stir-Fry

1½	**pounds fresh asparagus**
1	**tablespoon extra virgin olive oil**
2	**teaspoons sesame oil**
1	**tablespoon fresh ginger, finely chopped**
½	**cup unsalted cashews**
1	**tablespoon low-sodium soya sauce**

Cut the asparagus into 1-inch pieces.

In a skillet heat the oil and sesame oil. Stir in the ginger and cook 1 minute.

Add the asparagus and cook until tender.

Stir in the cashews and soya sauce, and cook for 1 to 2 minutes until heated.

MAKES 6 SERVINGS

Sautéed Zucchini and Tomatoes

3	**tablespoons extra virgin olive oil**
4	**medium zucchini, sliced**
1	**cup of tomato, chopped**
1	**clove of garlic, minced**
¹/₂	**teaspoon dried oregano**
¹/₂	**teaspoon dried basil**
	Fresh ground pepper

In a large skillet heat the olive oil. Add the zucchini and cook until tender crisp.

Add the tomato, garlic, oregano, basil, and pepper. Cook, stirring frequently, until the zucchini is tender.

MAKES 4 SERVINGS

Baked Yams

4	medium yams, peeled and sliced
1	cup unsweetened apple juice
2	teaspoons fresh gingerroot, grated
2	tablespoons honey

Preheat the oven to 425°.

In a large bowl combine the yams, apple juice, honey, and gingerroot. Bake uncovered for 30 minutes.

Serve immediately.

MAKES 4 SERVINGS

Garlic Broccoli with Balsamic Vinegar

4	tablespoons extra virgin olive oil
1	clove garlic, minced
1	bunch of broccoli, cut into florets
	Fresh ground pepper
1	tablespoon balsamic vinegar

Preheat the oven to 475°.

In a small bowl combine the olive oil and garlic.

Spread the broccoli on a baking sheet. Pour the garlic oil over the broccoli and toss to coat. Season with pepper. Roast 10 minutes, turning once.

Transfer to a serving dish and sprinkle with vinegar.

MAKES 4 SERVINGS

Fresh Asparagus with Lemon

1	bunch fresh asparagus
2	tablespoons extra virgin olive oil
2	teaspoons lemon pepper
1	tablespoon lemon juice
½	teaspoon grated lemon zest

Preheat the oven to 475°.

Spread the asparagus spears on a baking sheet. Pour the olive oil over the asparagus and season with the lemon pepper. Roast for 10 minutes, turning once.

Transfer to a serving dish. Toss with lemon juice and lemon zest.

MAKES 4 SERVINGS

Broccoli with Ginger

1	bunch of broccoli, broken into florets
2	tablespoons extra virgin olive oil
3	teaspoons fresh gingerroot, grated
1	tablespoon honey
2	tablespoons low-sodium soya sauce
¼	cup water
1	tablespoon cornstarch

Steam the broccoli for about 5 minutes or until tender.

In a medium skillet heat the olive oil and sauté the ginger for 1 minute. Stir in the broccoli and cook for 1 minute.

In a small bowl mix the honey and low-sodium soya sauce with the water. Pour over the broccoli and cook for another 5 minutes.

Stir in the cornstarch mixed with water and cook until thickened.

MAKES 6 SERVINGS

Marinated Tomatoes with Cilantro

4	medium tomatoes
1/4	cup chopped fresh cilantro
3	tablespoons extra virgin olive oil
1	tablespoon white wine vinegar
1	tablespoon red wine vinegar
1	tablespoon dried basil
1/2	teaspoon honey
	Fresh ground pepper

Slice the tomatoes and arrange on a serving dish. Sprinkle with cilantro.

In a small bowl whisk together, oil, red and white vinegar, basil, honey, and pepper. Pour over the tomatoes and chill for 1 hour.

MAKES 6 SERVINGS

Stir-Fried Leeks and Snow Peas

2	**large leeks**
2	**tablespoons extra virgin olive oil**
1	**medium onion, cut into rings**
2	**cloves garlic, minced**
½	**pound snow peas**
¼	**pound bean sprouts**
1	**tablespoon chopped fresh coriander**
	Fresh ground pepper

Trim the leeks and cut down the length of one side. Wash thoroughly. Cut the leeks into match-size pieces.

In a large skillet or wok heat the oil and sauté the onions and garlic for 2 minutes until the onions have softened.

Add the sliced leeks and snow peas, and stir-fry for 4 minutes.

Add the remaining ingredients and cook for 2 minutes. Serve.

Makes 4 servings

Dilly Cauliflower

1½	cups low-sodium chicken stock
2	bay leaves
1	teaspoon dill seeds
1	head cauliflower, cut into bite-size pieces
2	teaspoons Dijon mustard
1	teaspoon fresh dill

Pour the chicken stock into a large skillet. Add the dill seeds and bay leaves. Cover and simmer.

Add the cauliflower and simmer until tender.

Chill the cauliflower in its stock for 30 minutes.

Drain, reserving the stock, and place the cauliflower in a serving bowl.

Combine ½ cup of stock with the mustard. Drizzle over the cauliflower and sprinkle with fresh dill.

MAKES 6 SERVINGS

Spinach with Lemon Butter

1	**pound fresh spinach, cleaned and trimmed**
2	**teaspoons lemon juice**
2	**teaspoons soya butter, melted**
	Pinch nutmeg
	Fresh ground pepper

Rinse the spinach. In a large saucepan cook the spinach over medium heat for 2 minutes until the leaves have wilted. Drain well.

Sprinkle with the lemon juice, butter, nutmeg, and pepper. Serve.

MAKES 4 SERVINGS

Sautéed Celery

1	bunch celery, cut into diagonal slices
2	tablespoons extra virgin olive oil
1	bay leaf
1	teaspoon dried thyme
	Fresh ground pepper

In a large skillet heat the olive oil and cook the celery and remaining ingredients for about 5 minutes.

Discard the bay leaf and serve.

MAKES 4 SERVINGS

Zucchini with Tomatoes

1	tablespoon extra virgin olive oil
½	cup onion, finely chopped
1	cup fresh tomatoes, chopped
3	cups of zucchini, cut into strips

In a large skillet heat the olive oil and sauté the onion until soft.

Add the tomatoes and zucchini. Cover and cook for 10 minutes. Serve.

MAKES 4 SERVINGS

Ginger Orange Squash

3	*cups peeled cubed squash*
6	*tablespoons orange juice*
2	*teaspoons soya butter*
1	*clove garlic, minced*
1	*teaspoon minced gingerroot*
	Fresh ground pepper

In a large skillet combine the squash, orange juice, soya butter, garlic, and ginger. Cover and cook over low heat until tender.

Season with pepper.

MAKES 4 SERVINGS

Baked Squash

3	**Acorn squash, cut in half with seeds removed**
2	**tablespoons soya butter**
2	**tablespoons honey**
	Fresh ground pepper
	Sprinkle of cinnamon

Preheat the oven to 375°.

Place a teaspoon of butter and honey into each squash half. Sprinkle with pepper and cinnamon. Place the squash in a baking dish and cover. Bake for 1 hour and 30 minutes, basting every 15 minutes.

MAKES 6 SERVINGS

Sautéed Cabbage with Caraway

1	cup of water
¾	cup sliced onion
4	cups grated cabbage
2	tablespoons extra virgin olive oil
1	tablespoon vinegar
2	tablespoons caraway seeds

In a large skillet combine the onion and water. Cover and simmer until soft.

Add the cabbage and stir. Simmer about 10 minutes until the cabbage is tender crisp.

Add the olive oil, vinegar, and caraway seeds, and stir-fry for about 5 minutes until coated.

MAKES 4 SERVINGS

Great Chicken Recipes

Sesame Chicken Stir-Fry

2	tablespoons hot water
3	tablespoons dry mustard
½	cup low-sodium soya sauce
2	tablespoons toasted sesame seeds
1	clove garlic, minced
2	tablespoons extra virgin olive oil
4	chicken breasts, cut into cubes
	Fresh ground pepper
1	tablespoon lemon juice
2	teaspoons toasted sesame seeds

In a blender combine the water and dry mustard, and blend well. Add the soya sauce, 2 tablespoons of sesame seeds, and garlic, and blend for 1 minute. Set aside.

In a large skillet heat the olive oil over medium heat. Add the chicken, season with pepper, and cook until the chicken is done.

Sprinkle with the lemon juice and 2 teaspoons of sesame seeds. Cook for 2 more minutes. Serve.

MAKES 4 SERVINGS

Chicken Chili

6	**boneless, skinless chicken breasts, cut into ½-inch pieces**
1	**cup finely chopped onion**
1	**cup finely chopped red onion**
2	**medium red bell peppers, chopped**
2	**cloves garlic, minced**
2	**15.5-ounce cans great northern beans, drained and rinsed**
1¾	**cups low-sodium chicken stock**
2	**4.5-ounce cans green chilies, drained and chopped**
¼	**teaspoon cumin**

Spray a large skillet with nonstick cooking spray. Add the chicken, onions, bell peppers, and garlic, and cook over medium heat until the chicken is done.

Add the remaining ingredients and bring to a boil. Reduce the heat and simmer for 10 to 15 minutes until the sauce thickens.

MAKES 6 SERVINGS

Poppy Seed Mustard Baked Chicken

8	chicken thighs or legs
4	tablespoons soya butter, melted
4	tablespoons Dijon mustard
4	tablespoons honey
2	tablespoons fresh lemon juice
1	teaspoon paprika
	Fresh ground pepper
3	tablespoons poppy seeds

Preheat the oven to 400°. Spray a baking sheet with nonstick cooking spray. Place the chicken on the prepared baking sheet.

In a large bowl combine the soya butter, Dijon mustard, honey, lemon juice, paprika, and pepper. Brush the mixture over the chicken. Bake at 400° for 15 minutes.

Turn the chicken over and brush with the remaining mustard mixture. Sprinkle with poppy seeds. Bake for 15 more minutes.

MAKES 4 SERVINGS

Lemon Sesame Chicken

4	boneless, skinless chicken breasts
½	cup low-fat plain yogurt
	Grated rind and juice of 1 lemon
2	teaspoons medium curry paste
1	tablespoon sesame seeds

With a sharp knife, make cuts in the chicken at intervals.

In a small bowl combine the yogurt, lemon rind, lemon juice, and curry paste to form a smooth mixture. Spoon the mixture over the chicken breasts and arrange them on a baking sheet.

Broil for about 15 minutes, turning once, until the chicken is brown and cooked. Sprinkle with sesame seeds a couple of minutes before taking out of the oven.

MAKES 4 SERVINGS

Tomato Chicken Casserole

2	tablespoons extra virgin olive oil
8	chicken thighs
1	medium red onion, sliced
2	garlic cloves, minced
1	large red bell pepper, sliced thinly
	Juice and rind of 1 small orange
1/2	cup low-sodium chicken stock
1	14-ounce can chopped tomatoes
1/2	cup thinly sliced sun-dried tomatoes
1	tablespoon chopped fresh thyme
	Fresh ground pepper

In a large skillet heat the olive oil over medium high heat and fry the chicken, turning once, until golden brown on both sides.

Transfer the chicken to a large pot. Drain the excess fat from the skillet, add the onion, garlic, and bell pepper, and sauté for 4 minutes. Transfer the mixture to the pot with the chicken. Add the orange juice and rind, chicken stock, canned tomatoes, and sun-dried tomatoes, and stir to combine. Bring to a boil. Reduce the heat, cover, and simmer over low heat for 1 hour, stirring occasionally.

Add the fresh thyme and pepper before serving.

MAKES 4 SERVINGS

Creamy Chicken Stroganoff

3	tablespoons extra virgin olive oil
2¹/₂	cups sliced fresh mushrooms
2	boneless, skinless chicken breasts, cut into strips
¹/₂	cup finely chopped onion
3	tablespoons spelt flour
	Fresh ground pepper
1	teaspoon paprika
1	teaspoon parsley flakes
1	tablespoon low-sodium beef bouillon powder
1¹/₂	cups water
1	cup fat-free sour cream
	Brown rice

In a large skillet heat the olive oil over medium heat. Add the mushroms, chicken, and onions, and cook until the chicken is done, turning once.

Blend in the flour, pepper, paprika, parsley flakes, and bouillon powder. Stir in the water. Bring to a boil and cook, stirring constantly, until the liquid thickens.

Stir in the sour cream and serve over brown rice.

MAKES 4 SERVINGS

Glazed Chicken with Julienne Vegetables

2	*tablespoons cornstarch*
1	*can low-sodium chicken broth*
¼	*cup apple juice*
1	*tablespoon honey*
2	*tablespoons Dijon mustard*
2	*tablespoons extra virgin olive oil*
4	*skinless, boneless chicken breasts*
1	*large carrot, cut into thin strips*
1	*medium red bell pepper, cut into thin strips*

In a small bowl stir together the cornstarch, broth, apple juice, honey, and mustard and set aside.

In a large skillet heat half the oil and brown the chicken. Set aside. In the same skillet heat the remaining oil and stir-fry the carrot and pepper until tender crisp.

Stir in the reserved cornstarch mixture. Cook until the mixture boils and thickens.

Add the chicken and coat with the glaze. Serve.

MAKES 4 SERVINGS

Stir-Fry Chicken with Broccoli

2	tablespoons low-sodium soya sauce
2	cloves garlic, minced
¼	cup low-sodium chicken broth
4	boneless, skinless chicken breasts, cut into strips
1	head broccoli, cut into bite-size pieces
2	carrots, cut into strips
1	large onion, cut into large slices
1	teaspoon Oriental sesame oil

In a medium bowl combine the soya sauce, garlic, and 2 tablespoons of chicken broth. Add the chicken to the broth mixture.

In a large nonstick skillet cook the chicken with the broth mixture for 5 minutes.

Remove the chicken with a slotted spoon, leaving the liquid in the skillet.

Add the broccoli, carrots, onion, and remaining broth. Cover and cook for 4 minutes.

Add the chicken and stir-fry for 2 minutes. Sprinkle with oil and serve.

MAKES 4 SERVINGS

Red Lentil Chicken Curry

¹/₂	cup red lentils, rinsed
2	tablespoons curry powder
2	teaspoons ground coriander
1	teaspoon cumin seeds
2	cups vegetable stock
8	skinless chicken thighs
8	ounces fresh spinach, cleaned well
1	tablespoon chopped fresh cilantro
	Ground pepper to taste

In a large saucepan place the lentils, curry powder, coriander, cumin seeds, and vegetable stock. Bring to a boil. Reduce the heat, cover, and simmer for 10 minutes.

Add the chicken and spinach and simmer for 50 minutes or until the chicken is done.

Stir in the cilantro and pepper to taste. Serve.

MAKES 4 SERVINGS

Garlic Chicken Breasts

4	**boneless, skinless chicken breasts**
½	**cup spelt flour**
1	**tablespoon extra virgin olive oil**
4	**cloves garlic, minced**
½	**cup low-sodium chicken broth**
3	**tablespoons balsamic vinegar**
	Fresh ground pepper
1	**tablespoon water**
2	**teaspoons cornstarch**

Dredge the chicken breasts in flour.

In a large skillet heat the oil over medium heat. Add the chicken breasts and cook for 3 minutes. Add the garlic and cook until the chicken is golden.

Add the broth, vinegar, and pepper. Cover and cook at medium heat for 10 minutes, or until the chicken is tender.

Remove the chicken from the skillet.

In a small bowl mix the cornstarch and water. Add the cornstarch mixture to the skillet and bring to a boil. Cook, stirring constantly, until thickened.

Pour the sauce over the chicken and enjoy.

MAKES 4 SERVINGS

Honey Glazed Chicken

¼	cup spelt flour
	Fresh ground pepper
4	boneless, skinless chicken breasts
3	tablespoons honey
2	tablespoons Dijon mustard
1	tablespoon extra virgin olive oil

Preheat the oven to 350°. In a shallow dish combine the flour and pepper. Dredge the chicken breasts with the flour mixture.

In a small bowl combine the honey and mustard.

In a medium skillet heat the olive oil over medium heat and brown the chicken on both sides.

Place the chicken on a baking sheet and spread the honey mixture over the chicken.

Bake at 350° for 15 minutes or until tender.

MAKES 4 SERVINGS

Chicken Breasts with Toasted Sesame Seeds

4	**boneless, skinless chicken breasts**
3	**tablespoons extra virgin olive oil**
$\frac{1}{2}$	**cup unsweetened apple juice**
4	**tablespoons chopped green onion**
4	**tablespoons toasted sesame seeds**

In a large skillet heat the oil and brown the chicken on both sides for about 5 minutes.

Add the onion and apple juice. Simmer for about 20 minutes or until the chicken is cooked.

Place the chicken on a serving platter and spoon the remaining juices over the chicken. Sprinkle with sesame seeds.

MAKES 4 SERVINGS

Baked Chicken Breasts in Yogurt Sauce

6	boneless, skinless chicken breasts
¼	cup low-sodium chicken stock
3	tablespoons Parmesan cheese
1½	tablespoons prepared mustard
1	teaspoon thyme
1	cup low-fat plain yogurt
2	tablespoons spelt flour

Preheat the oven to 350°.

Arrange the chicken breasts in a casserole dish. In a small bowl combine the cheese, mustard, thyme, and chicken stock. Stir well.

In a medium bowl mix the yogurt and flour together. Add the cheese mixture. Stir. Spoon the sauce over chicken fillets. Bake uncovered at 350° for 1 hour or until the chicken is cooked.

MAKES 6 SERVINGS

Chicken and Sweet Pepper Sauté

2	teaspoons extra virgin olive oil
4	boneless, skinless, chicken breasts
1	red bell pepper, seeded and cut into 1-inch pieces
1	yellow bell pepper, seeded and cut into 1- inch pieces
1	medium zucchini, sliced
	Fresh ground pepper
¼	cup low-sodium chicken broth
4	teaspoons balsamic vinegar

In a large skillet heat 1½ teaspoons of olive oil over medium heat. Add the chicken and cook until tender and browned on both sides. Remove to a platter.

To the skillet add the remaining ½ teaspoon olive oil, peppers, zucchini, and pepper, and sauté until tender, stirring frequently.

Add the chicken broth and balsamic vinegar, and bring to a boil.

Pour the sauce over the chicken.

MAKES 4 SERVINGS

Fibro-Fish Dishes

Broiled Flounder with Fresh Basil

¼	cup extra virgin olive oil
1	tablespoon lemon juice
1	teaspoon chopped fresh basil
	Fresh ground pepper
4	flounder fillets

In a small bowl mix the oil, lemon juice, basil, and pepper.

Place the fish fillets in a broiling pan and broil, basting generously with the oil mixture, for 8 minutes or until the fish flakes with fork.

MAKES 4 SERVINGS

Broiled Tarragon Flounder

¼	**cup extra virgin olive oil**
1	**tablespoon lemon juice**
1	**teaspoon chopped fresh tarragon**
	Fresh ground pepper
4	**flounder fillets**

In a small bowl mix the oil, lemon juice, tarragon and pepper.

Place the fish fillets in a broiling pan and broil, basting generously with the oil mixture, for 8 minutes or until the fish flakes with fork.

MAKES 4 SERVINGS

Cod with Horseradish Mayonnaise

6	tablespoons low-fat mayonnaise
1	clove garlic, finely chopped
1	tablespoon chopped fresh cilantro
2	teaspoons horseradish
1	teaspoon grated lemon rind
	Fresh ground pepper
4	cod fillets

In a small bowl combine the mayonnaise, garlic, cilantro, horseradish, lemon rind, and pepper.

Grease a broiling pan and place the fish on the pan. Spread the mayonnaise mixture on each fillet. Broil 4 inches from heat for 6 minutes or until the fish is cooked through.

MAKES 4 SERVINGS

Curry Shrimp Skewers

1	pound large shrimp
4	teaspoons extra extra virgin olive oil
1	teaspoon curry paste
¼	cup finely chopped fresh coriander

Peel and de-vein the shrimp. Rinse and pat dry.

In a large bowl stir the oil and curry paste together. Add the shrimp and coat evenly. Cover and refrigerate overnight.

Place 4 shrimps onto each of 10 skewers.

Place on an oven rack and bake at 375°, turning once, for about 5 minutes, until pink.

Transfer to a serving tray. Sprinkle with fresh chopped coriander and serve.

MAKES 6 SERVINGS

Edwina's Baked Salmon

4	**salmon fillets**
¼	**cup low-fat mayonnaise**
¼	**teaspoon pepper**
½	**teaspoon garlic powder**
¼	**teaspoon dill weed**

Place the salmon fillets on greased foil, skin side down. Spread with mayonnaise. Sprinkle with the pepper, dill weed, and garlic powder. Fold the foil over the salmon sealing, completely.

Bake at 450° for 10 to 15 minutes or until the fish flakes when tested with a fork.

MAKES 4 SERVINGS

Easy Sole Casserole

2	tablespoons extra virgin olive oil
1	cup cleaned and sliced fresh mushrooms
2	green onions, sliced
$^1/_2$	teaspoon dried parsley flakes
1	teaspoon dill weed
4	sole fillets, cut into bite-size pieces
$^1/_4$	cup fat-free sour cream
6	tablespoons low-fat mayonnaise
2	tablespoons spelt flour
	Fresh ground pepper
	Sprinkle of paprika

TOPPING	
2	tablespoons soya butter
$^1/_2$	cup dried brown breadcrumbs

In a medium skillet heat the olive oil and sauté the mushrooms and onions until tender. Transfer the mushroom mixture to a 2-quart casserole dish and add the parsley and dill. Arrange the fish over the mushroom mixture.

In a small bowl combine the sour cream, mayonnaise, flour, pepper, and paprika. Spread the mixture over the fish.

In a small skillet melt the butter and stir in the breadcrumbs. Stir to coat. Sprinkle the breadcrumbs over the casserole. Bake at 375° for 30 minutes or until the fish is done.

MAKES 4 SERVINGS

Fillet of Sole with Almonds

½	cup spelt flour
1	teaspoon lemon pepper
4	sole fillets
2	tablespoons soya butter
2	tablespoons extra virgin olive oil
½	cup sliced almonds
2	tablespoons fresh lemon juice
1	tablespoon chopped fresh parsley

On a plate combine the flour and lemon pepper. Dip the fish fillets in the seasoned flour to coat.

In a large skillet heat 1 tablespoon of olive oil and 1 tablespoon of soya butter over medium heat. Add the fish and cook, turning once, until lightly browned. Remove the fish to a serving plate.

Reduce the heat to medium-low and add the remaining butter and oil. Add the almonds and cook for 2 to 3 minutes. Stir in the lemon juice and parsley. Spoon the almond mixture over the fish.

MAKES 4 SERVINGS

Flounder with Horseradish and Parsley Mayonnaise

6	tablespoons low-fat mayonnaise
1	clove of garlic, minced
2	tablespoons chopped fresh parsley
2	teaspoons of horseradish
1	teaspoon lemon rind, grated
	Fresh ground pepper
4	flounder fillets

In a small bowl combine all of the ingredients except the fish. Mix together well.

Preheat the broiler.

Grease the broiling pan and place the fish on the pan. Spread the mayonnaise mixture on each fillet.

Broil for 4 to 5 minutes or until the fish is fully cooked and the top is browned.

MAKES 4 SERVINGS

Ginger Shrimp

2	tablespoons extra virgin olive oil
1½	pounds fresh shrimp, peeled and cleaned
1	inch of fresh gingerroot, finely chopped
2	cloves garlic, finely chopped
2	green onions, finely chopped
½	cup fresh peas, shelled
1	leek, white part only, cut into strips
¾	cup fresh bean sprouts
2	tablespoons low-sodium soya sauce
1	teaspoon honey

In a large skillet or wok heat the oil and stir-fry the shrimp for 2 minutes. Set aside.

Reheat the oil and add the ginger and garlic. Add the onions, peas, and leeks. Stir-fry for 3 minutes.

Add the bean sprouts and shrimp to the cooked vegetables. Stir in the honey and low-sodium soya sauce. Cook for 2 minutes and serve immediately.

MAKES 6 SERVINGS

Orange Roughy with Orange Lime Sauce

4	orange roughy fillets
½	cup skim milk
6	tablespoons spelt flour
2	tablespoons extra virgin olive oil
1	clove garlic, minced
3	tablespoons lime juice
2	tablespoons orange juice
2	tablespoons finely chopped parsley
1	green onion, finely chopped
1	tablespoon soya butter

Soak the fillets in milk for 15 minutes.

Dredge the fish in flour, shaking off the excess.

In a large skillet heat the olive oil and add the fish. Cook until golden brown. Remove the fish to a serving platter.

In a medium skillet at low temperature, heat 1 teaspoon of olive oil, add the garlic, and sauté 1 minute. Add the lime and orange juice, parsley, and onion. Add the soya butter and blend well until creamy. Pour the sauce over the fish fillets and serve.

MAKES 4 SERVINGS

Scallops with Citrus Sauce

1	tablespoon extra virgin olive oil
1	small onion, finely chopped
2	cups of large scallops
2	tablespoons grated orange rind
	Fresh ground pepper
1	teaspoon dried tarragon
$1/4$	cup orange juice
1	tablespoon lemon juice
$3/4$	cup non-fat sour cream
1	tablespoon grated lemon rind

In a large skillet heat the olive oil and sauté the onion until tender. Add the scallops, orange rind, pepper, and tarragon, and sauté for 2 minutes.

Add the orange juice and lemon juice, and simmer for 1 minute.

Reduce the heat and stir in the sour cream and lemon rind. Simmer, stirring constantly, for 5 minutes or until the sauce thickens.

Serve with rice or pasta.

MAKES 6 SERVINGS

Scallops with Lemon Pepper Butter

¼	**cup spelt flour**
1	**teaspoon lemon pepper**
1	**cup of fresh scallops**
4	**tablespoons soya butter**
1	**tablespoon fresh lemon juice**
1	**tablespoon chopped fresh parsley**

In a small bowl combine the flour and lemon pepper. Dredge the scallops in the flour mixture.

In a large skillet melt 2 tablespoons of soya butter over medium heat. Add the scallops and cook until golden brown. Remove to a plate.

Reduce the heat, return the skillet to the heat, and melt the remaining butter. Whisk in the lemon juice and parsley. Spoon over the scallops and serve.

MAKES 4 SERVINGS

Sole with Garlic Lemon Butter

3	tablespoons soya butter
2	cloves garlic, minced
2	tablespoons fresh parsley, minced
½	teaspoon lemon rind
4	sole fillets
2	tablespoons fresh lemon juice

In a small bowl cream the butter, and blend in the garlic, parsley, and lemon rind. Pat the fish dry. Arrange the fish in a well-greased broiling pan. Sprinkle with lemon juice. Spread with the butter mixture. Broil for 7 minutes or until the fish flakes with fork.

MAKES 4 SERVINGS

Tomato Baked Cod Fillets

4	**cod fillets**
4	**fresh tomatoes cut in half**
$^1/_2$	**teaspoon grated lemon rind**
	Fresh ground pepper
1	**teaspoon oregano**
1	**tablespoon chopped fresh chives**
$^1/_2$	**teaspoon dill weed**
2	**tablespoons soya butter, melted**

Preheat the oven to 400°. Lightly spray a shallow baking pan with non-stick cooking spray.

Rinse the fish and pat dry. Arrange the fish in a pan and place tomato halves around the fish. Sprinkle the lemon rind, pepper, oregano, chives, and dill weed over the fish. Drizzle with the melted soya butter. Bake, uncovered, for 20 minutes.

MAKES 4 SERVINGS

Tuna Steaks with Ginger

1	tablespoon orange rind
1/4	cup low-sodium soya sauce
1	garlic clove, minced
1	teaspoon chopped fresh ginger
3/4	cup fresh orange juice
1	tablespoon lemon juice
2	tuna steaks

In a shallow baking dish combine the orange rind, soya sauce, garlic, ginger, and citrus juices.

Marinate the tuna steaks for 20 minutes. Grill the tuna for 5 minutes on each side, basting with the marinade.

MAKES 2 SERVINGS

Dressings

Yogurt Salad Dressing

1	cup low-fat plain yogurt
2	tablespoons white vinegar
1½	tablespoons lemon juice
	Fresh ground pepper
2	tablespoons finely chopped chives
2	tablespoons finely chopped parsley

In a small bowl combine all of the ingredients and blend well. Refrigerate.

Serve over favorite salad greens.

Honey Mustard Salad Dressing

$\frac{1}{2}$	**cup non-fat yogurt**
$\frac{1}{2}$	**cup low-fat mayonnaise**
2	**tablespoons lemon juice**
$\frac{1}{4}$	**cup honey**
1	**teaspoon dry mustard**

In a small bowl combine all of the ingredients and blend well. Refrigerate.

Serve over favorite salad greens.

Tarragon Dressing

1/2	cup fat-free sour cream
1/4	cup low-fat mayonnaise
1/4	cup skim milk
1	tablespoon tarragon vinegar
1/4	teaspoon fresh leaf tarragon, crumbled
	Fresh ground pepper

In a small bowl combine all of the ingredients and blend well.

Serve over favorite salad greens.

Creamy Orange Dressing

1/4	cup fat-free sour cream
1/4	cup low-fat mayonnaise
2	teaspoons grated orange rind
1/4	cup orange juice
1	tablespoon lemon juice

In a small bowl combine all of the ingredients and blend well. Cover and refrigerate for up to one day.
Serve over favorite salad greens.

Curry Salad Dressing

2	tablespoons vinegar
1	tablespoon lemon juice
2	teaspoons curry powder
1	teaspoon honey
½	low-fat cream
½	cup fat-free sour cream

In a small bowl combine all of the ingredients and blend well.

Serve over favorite salad greens.

Sunflower Seed Salad Dressing

½	**cup unsalted sunflower seeds**
1	**garlic clove**
	Fresh ground pepper
1	**tablespoon chopped fresh parsley**
1	**cup plain non-fat yogurt**

In a blender process the sunflower seeds. Add the garlic, pepper, lemon juice, and yogurt to the sunflower seeds and blend until smooth.

Serve as a dip or over favorite salad greens.

Herbed French Dressing

1	cup extra virgin olive oil
¼	cup wine vinegar
½	teaspoon seasoned pepper
½	teaspoon garlic powder
¼	teaspoon dried basil leaves
¼	teaspoon dried oregano leaves
¼	teaspoon paprika

In a jar combine all of the ingredients, cover, and shake to combine. Refrigerate.

Serve over favorite salad greens.

Poppy Seed Dressing

3	tablespoons extra virgin olive oil
1	tablespoon fresh lime juice
1½	tablespoons honey
1	tablespoon water
1	tablespoon poppy seeds
1	teaspoon grated orange peel

In a small bowl whisk together all of the ingredients. Serve with favorite fresh fruit or salad greens.

Yogurt Vinaigrette

2	*tablespoons white wine vinegar*
2	*tablespoons fresh lemon juice*
1	*garlic clove, minced*
1	*teaspoon Dijon mustard*
	Fresh ground pepper
¾	*cup plain low-fat yogurt*
2	*tablespoons extra virgin olive oil*
2	*tablespoons chopped fresh tarragon*

In a small bowl combine the vinegar, lemon juice, garlic, mustard, pepper, and yogurt. Stir well. Stir in the olive oil and tarragon.

Serve over favorite salad greens.

Lemon Honey Dressing

¹/₂	cup low-fat mayonnaise
¹/₂	cup non-fat yogurt
1¹/₂	teaspoons lemon juice
¹/₄	cup honey
¹/₂	teaspoon dry mustard
¹/₄	teaspoon celery seed

In a small bowl combine all of the ingredients and blend well. Refrigerate.

Serve over favorite salad greens.

Sauces and Dips

Red Bell Pepper Dip

1	**red onion, unpeeled, halved**
4	**large red bell peppers**
3	**large cloves garlic, unpeeled**
¼	**cup walnuts**
3	**tablespoons Parmesan cheese**
2	**tablespoons red wine vinegar**

Preheat the oven to 500°.

Line a cookie sheet with foil. Place the onion and peppers on the pan. Bake for 20 minutes. Halfway through cooking, add the garlic and turn the peppers over.

Remove from the pan. Wrap the peppers, onions, and garlic in foil, sealing well. Let stand for 10 minutes.

Peel the peppers and take out the seeds. Peel the garlic and onion. Place in a blender; add the walnuts, Parmesan cheese, and vinegar. Blend until the mixture is smooth. Chill.

Serve with raw veggies.

Great Northern Bean Dip

1	**15.8-ounce can great northern beans, drained**
2	**teaspoons minced fresh thyme**
2	**teaspoons balsamic vinegar**
1	**teaspoon extra virgin olive oil**
½	**teaspoon dry mustard**
½	**teaspoon ground pepper**
2	**tablespoons minced fresh parsley**

In a medium bowl combine the beans, thyme, vinegar, olive oil, dry mustard, and pepper. Mix with a potato masher until smooth. Stir in the parsley.

Transfer the dip to a serving bowl, cover, and chill for 1 hour.

Serve with raw veggies.

Creamy Cucumber Dill Sauce

1	medium cucumber, peeled, seeded, and shredded
1	cup fat-free sour cream
3	tablespoons low-fat mayonnaise
1	teaspoon dill weed
1	teaspoon lemon juice
	Fresh ground pepper

In a small bowl, combine all of the ingredients. Cover and refrigerate for 1 hour.

Bring to room temperature before serving. Spoon over grilled fish.

Creamy Parsley Sauce

³/₄	**cup fat-free sour cream**
¹/₂	**cup low-fat mayonnaise**
¹/₂	**teaspoon lemon juice**
1	**tablespoon chopped chives**
2	**teaspoons parsley flakes**
1	**teaspoon dill weed**
1	**teaspoon horseradish**
¹/₂	**teaspoon Worcestershire sauce**

In a medium bowl mix together all of the ingredients. Heat the sauce before serving over your favorite fish fillets.

Pesto Sauce

2	cups packed fresh basil leaves
1/2	cup extra virgin olive oil
2	tablespoons soya butter
1/4	cup pine nuts
3	large cloves garlic
	Fresh ground pepper
1/2	cup fresh grated Parmesan cheese

In a food processor combine the basil, oil, soya butter, pine nuts, garlic, and pepper and process until puréed. Transfer to a medium bowl. Stir in the cheese. Cover and refrigerate for up to 3 days.

Pesto sauce goes great with poached, grilled, or baked fish fillets.

Fruit Dip

1	cup low-fat yogurt
1	tablespoon honey
	Pinch nutmeg
	Pinch allspice

In a small bowl combine all of the ingredients. Refrigerate.

Serve with fresh fruit.

Zucchini Dip

3	cups shredded zucchini
¼	cup finely chopped fresh cilantro
3	tablespoons red wine vinegar
1	tablespoon extra virgin olive oil
2	cloves garlic, minced
	Fresh ground pepper
3	tablespoons finely chopped pecans

Remove the excess water from the shredded zucchini. Place the zucchini, cilantro, vinegar, olive oil, garlic, and pepper in a blender and process until smooth. Spoon the mixture into a serving bowl and sprinkle with pecans. Chill before serving.

Dill Dip

½	cup low-fat mayonnaise
¾	cup non-fat sour cream
1	tablespoon onion flakes
2	teaspoons parsley flakes
2	teaspoons dill weed
½	teaspoon paprika

In a medium bowl mix all of the ingredients. Chill before serving with favorite raw veggies.

Dill Dip 2

½	**cup low-fat mayonnaise**
¾	**cup non-fat sour cream**
2	**teaspoons onion flakes**
3	**teaspoons dill weed**
½	**teaspoon celery salt**

In a medium bowl combine all of the ingredients. Chill before serving with raw veggies.

Fruit

Fresh Fruit Topping

½	**cup plain low-fat yogurt**
½	**cup low-fat cottage cheese**
3	**tablespoons honey**
1	**teaspoon vanilla extract**

In a blender process all ingredients until creamy. Cover and refrigerate.

Serve over fresh fruit.

MAKES 6 SERVINGS

Fresh Mangoes with Yogurt

3	**cups sliced fresh mangoes**
8	**ounces plain low-fat yogurt**
1	**teaspoon ground cinnamon**

Spoon the fruit into chilled fruit bowls. Top with yogurt and sprinkle with cinnamon.

MAKES 4 SERVINGS

Fresh Strawberries with Toasted Coconut

2	**cups fresh strawberries**
¼	**cup low-fat vanilla yogurt**
2	**tablespoons unsweetened coconut**

Rinse and clean the berries. Place the berries in a small bowl. Stir in the yogurt. Sprinkle with coconut.

MAKES 2 TO 4 SERVINGS

Banana Yogurt

2	cups chopped bananas
1	teaspoon grated orange rind
1	tablespoon lemon juice
2	tablespoons honey
1	cup low-fat plain yogurt

In a blender place the bananas, orange rind, lemon juice, honey, and yogurt. Blend until smooth. Chill before serving.

MAKES 4 SERVINGS

Peach Yogurt

2	cups chopped fresh peaches
1	teaspoon grated orange rind
1	tablespoon lemon juice
2	tablespoons honey
1	cup low-fat plain yogurt

In a blender place the chopped peaches, orange rind, lemon juice, honey, and yogurt. Blend until smooth. Chill before serving.

MAKES 4 SERVINGS

Rice and Pasta

Rice Pilaf

2	teaspoons soya butter
¾	cup chopped pecans
¼	cup finely chopped onions
1	cup uncooked brown basmati rice
2	cups low-sodium chicken broth
1	teaspoon dried thyme
1	tablespoon chopped fresh parsley
	Fresh ground pepper

Preheat the oven to 325°.

In a medium skillet melt 1 teaspoon of soya butter over medium heat. Add the pecans and sauté for 2 minutes. Remove from the skillet and set aside.

In the same skillet melt the remaining soya butter and sauté the onion until transparent. Add the rice to the onion and stir. Add the chicken broth, thyme, pepper, and parsley. Cover and bring to a boil.

Pour into an ovenproof casserole and bake uncovered until the liquid is absorbed, about 15 minutes or until the rice is cooked.

Before serving, stir in the pecans.

MAKES 6 SERVINGS

Cilantro Basmati Brown Rice

2	tablespoons extra virgin olive oil
½	cup finely chopped onion
1	tablespoon finely chopped fresh cilantro
	Dash turmeric
1	cup brown basmati rice

In a medium skillet heat the oil and sauté the onion until tender. Add the cilantro and turmeric. Stir and set aside.

In a separate pot cook the rice according to the package directions. Stir the onion mixture into the hot rice.

MAKES 4 SERVINGS

Mushroom Pasta Casserole

2	tablespoons extra virgin olive oil
1	clove garlic, minced
$^1/_2$	teaspoon basil
$^1/_2$	teaspoon thyme
$^1/_2$	teaspoon paprika
1	teaspoon low-sodium soya sauce
$1^1/_2$	pounds fresh mushrooms, sliced
$3^1/_2$	ounces Parmesan cheese, grated
4	cups of pasta sauce
1	package rice spaghetti pasta

In a large skillet heat the oil and sauté the garlic. Add the basil, thyme, paprika, soya sauce, and mushrooms, and sauté for 15 minutes over low heat.

In a casserole dish place the mushroom mixture and sprinkle with Parmesan cheese. Cover with pasta sauce. Cover and bake at 350° for 30 minutes.

Meanwhile cook the pasta according to the package directions and drain.

Serve the mushroom casserole over the pasta.

MAKES 6 SERVINGS

Pasta with Mushroom Sauce

½	**pound fresh mushrooms**
2	**tablespoons soya butter**
2	**tablespoons spelt flour**
1	**cup skim milk**
½	**cup fat-free sour cream**
1	**teaspoon ground thyme**
	Fresh ground pepper
1½	**cups brown rice pasta shells**

Clean the mushrooms and chop coarsely.

In a small saucepan melt the butter and add the mushrooms. Sauté for 5 minutes.

Stir in the flour and cook 1 minute, stirring constantly. Add the milk, sour cream, thyme, and pepper, stirring constantly. Bring to a boil and cook for 3 minutes.

In a medium saucepan cook the pasta in water until tender. Rinse and drain.

Pour the mushroom sauce over the pasta and serve immediately.

MAKES 4 SERVINGS

Pasta with Basil Sauce

1	pound rice pasta, any shape
4	tablespoons extra virgin olive oil
2	cloves garlic, minced
4	medium tomatoes, peeled, seeded, and finely chopped
	Fresh ground pepper
10	fresh basil leaves, finely chopped

Cook the pasta in boiling water, rinse, and set aside.

In a medium skillet heat the olive oil and cook the garlic and tomatoes with pepper over medium heat for 10 minutes.

Stir the well-drained pasta into the skillet and mix well until heated.

Sprinkle chopped basil leaves over the pasta before serving.

MAKES 4 SERVINGS

Pasta with Pesto Sauce

2	**cups rice pasta**
2	**cups fresh basil**
3	**tablespoons pine nuts**
3	**cloves garlic, chopped**
	Fresh ground pepper
½	**cup extra virgin olive oil**
¼	**cup Parmesan cheese**

In a large pot of boiling water cook the pasta until tender. Drain and return to the pot.

In a blender, blend the basil, pine nuts, garlic, and pepper until smooth.

Slowly add the olive oil and Parmesan cheese, blending well.

Pour the pesto sauce over the pasta and coat well.

MAKES 6 SERVINGS

Breads

Banana Bread

3	ripe bananas, mashed
	Juice of 1 lemon
$\frac{1}{2}$	cup honey
$\frac{1}{2}$	cup soya butter
$1\frac{3}{4}$	cups spelt flour
$\frac{1}{4}$	cup rice bran
1	teaspoon cinnamon
$\frac{1}{2}$	teaspoon baking powder
$\frac{1}{2}$	teaspoon baking soda
$\frac{3}{4}$	cup chopped walnuts

Preheat the oven to 375°.

In a small bowl add the lemon juice to the mashed bananas and mix until smooth.

In a large bowl mix the butter and honey together. Add the banana mixture and blend together.

In a separate bowl mix the flour, rice bran, cinnamon, baking powder, and baking soda together. Fold in the walnuts. Add the dry ingredients to the liquid mixture, stirring just until blended. Pour into greased loaf pan and bake for 40 minutes.

Let cool before cutting.

MAKES 1 LOAF

Blueberry Muffins

3	**cups Spelt Pancake and Muffin Mix**
½	**cup honey**
½	**cup fresh blueberries**
1	**cup skim milk**

Preheat the oven to 400°.

In a medium bowl mix all of the ingredients together until blended well. Grease the muffin tins and spoon the batter into them. Bake for 20 minutes and let cool.

MAKES 12 MUFFINS

$\mathcal{S}$pelt $\mathcal{B}$read

3	cups warm water
1	tablespoon honey
2	tablespoons dry, granulated yeast
4	cups fine spelt flour, divided
3	cups spelt flour

In a large bowl dissolve the honey and yeast in warm water and stir in 1 cup fine flour. Set the bowl in a sink with very warm water until the liquid bubbles, about 15 minutes.

Using an electric mixer, beat in the remaining 3 cups of fine flour on low speed. When the flour is moist, continue beating on medium speed for 3 minutes. Gradually stir the remaining 3 cups of flour into the dough, using a large spoon. Turn the dough out on a floured board and knead for 10 minutes.

Oil a large bowl. Place the dough in it and turn once to grease the top surface of the dough. Cover with a tea towel and set in a warm place to rise.

When the dough is double in size, punch it down and knead briefly right in the bowl for 2 minutes. Cover and return to a warm place for 1 hour.

Knead on a lightly floured surface, divide and shape into 2 loaves. Divide and place in oiled and floured loaf pans. Cover with a towel and put in a warm place to let the bread rise to the top of the pans.

Preheat the oven to 425°. Remove the towel and place the bread in the oven. Bake for 15 minutes. Reduce the heat to 350° and bake for 30 minutes more.

Remove the loaves from the pans and lay on their sides on wire racks to cool.

MAKES 2 LOAVES

Spelt Muffins

2 ¼	cups spelt flour
1	tablespoon baking powder
1¼	cups skim milk
3	eggs, beaten
¼	cup honey
1	tablespoon extra virgin olive oil
½	cup chopped nuts (optional)

In a large bowl combine the flour and baking powder. Add the milk, eggs, honey, and oil. Mix well. Add nuts if desired. Fill paper muffin cups. Bake at 375° for 17 minutes.

MAKES 6 LARGE MUFFINS

Spelt Pie Crust

3	*tablespoons extra virgin olive oil*
2	*tablespoons cool water*
1	*cup + 2 tablespoons spelt flour*

In a medium bowl combine the water and oil, and mix well. Stir in the flour and mix until evenly moistened. Press into a pie plate. Fill and bake at 350° for 15 minutes.

Index

P

R

S

Y

Z

About the Author

Shelley Ann Smith is a pharmacy technician who suffers from fibromyalgia. She has studied the ways in which proper eating and health habits can provide relief from the symptoms of the disease. The mother of four children, she lives in Barrie, Ontario, Canada.